learn to play Tennis AT HOME

DeWitt Willis

McGraw-Hill Book Company

New York   St. Louis   San Francisco   Auckland   Düsseldorf   Johannesburg
Kuala Lumpur   London   Mexico   Montreal   New Delhi   Panama
Paris   São Paulo   Singapore   Sydney   Tokyo   Toronto

Graphic Concepts and Book Design by Rosemary Lois.
Photography by Carl Fischer.

1 2 3 4 5 6 7 8 9 DO DO 7 9 8 7 6

Library of Congress Cataloging in Publication Data

Willis, DeWitt.
   Learn to play tennis at home.

   (McGraw-Hill paperbacks)
   SUMMARY: The author presents his system, "Rhythmetonics," a method of learning and perfecting tennis techniques at home so that the movements will be fixed in one's memory before even approaching the court.
   1. Tennis.   [1. Tennis]   I. Title.
GV995.W69 796.34'22 76-5941
ISBN 0-07-070625-5

INTRODUCTION

Almost everyone you talk with today is either a serious tennis player, is just learning to play, or is considering taking up the sport. It has always been my opinion that the game would enjoy a phenomenal growth so, to me, its present popularity is long overdue. After all, tennis does not require a great deal of time, expense or people, and it is the sport of a lifetime. As a matter of fact, it has been a major part of my life and as a player, Davis Cup Captain and U.S. Open Tournament Director, as well as a conductor of numerous exhibitions and clinics, I can tell you that tennis challenges not only the body—demanding healthy exercise and muscle development—but the mind as well, requiring mental alertness to devise and execute strategies and strokes necessary to win a game. With regular practice and concentration, I am convinced everyone can develop a certain degree of expertise in tennis.

A comprehensive, easily understood book on how to play the game, with tennis tips and techniques, is essential both for the novice and the more devoted player. *Learn to Play Tennis at Home* is a unique book which allows you to do exactly what the title suggests. From the carefully presented exercises, you will learn the elements of good tennis before getting out on a court or hitting a ball. The theory here that perhaps a more effective way to learn the game is to perfect smooth strokes before going out on the court is a logical concept that DeWitt Willis has carefully and thoroughly outlined. Whenever you wish to develop or improve a stroke or where court time and space are limited, you will find this book indispensable.

I wish it had been available when I was first learning the game, but even today, 44 years later, I can still utilize DeWitt Willis' helpful hints to make certain my strokes are properly executed.

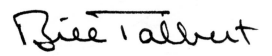

PREFACE

Most likely the immediate reaction to the RHYTHMETONICS exercise method of teaching tennis will be "What is RHYTHMETONICS?" "What is the value of RHYTHMETONICS as a fundamental method of learning tennis?"

As an orthopedic surgeon and ex-athlete, I reacted that way. However, after a few minutes of explanation by tennis pro DeWitt Willis, the answers were obvious, and I found that I not only agreed with the principle, but endorsed it fully.

Mr. Willis presents the correct stance, arm movements, body turns and pivots that are required to play tennis smoothly with supple coordination. His art is to teach perfection. He accomplishes this in several ways. Students who follow Mr. Willis through his continuous flow of turns, swings and pivots will establish within themselves a feeling tone or body knowledge of each position, each turn and each movement of the racquet. In doing so, the correct position, movement, and muscular balance and all the correct steps and swings that are required in the game of tennis will be fixed in the conscious and unconscious memory. Students learn to think, move, stand, and swing the DeWitt Willis way.

The RHYTHMETONICS method can be applied to other sports as well; let us look at some statements often made by great professional athletes. "I knew when the ball left my hands, it was going to be a basket!" "I knew the second I hit the ball, we could add a home run to our score." "I knew when my toe struck the ball, it was good for three points." What are these athletes saying?

Each act was performed with a perfection the athletes knew to be true from their body knowledge, or the feeling tone they received from their muscles. Technically, this knowledge is known as "proprioceptive sensibility." It is sometimes called position sense and is made possible by a nervous system which provides receptor end organs throughout the musculoskeletal system of the body. Position information is transmitted over long tract nerve fibers to the brain, where messages are recorded and appreciated by the conscious mind of the thoughtful and attentive athlete or student.

Repeated practice creates an awareness of the correct positions and body movements. If the student or athlete through proper training performs the positions, turns, pivots, arm movements and swings in precisely the correct way, he or she will be able to know, both from visual observation and from *body knowledge*, the correctness of a position as that position is attained. This is the essence of RHYTHMETONICS exercise as Mr. Willis presents it in the teaching of tennis.

RUSSELL O. GEE, M.D.
Orthopedic Surgeon

CONTENTS

Chapter 1
LEARNING AT HOME

I've hit 3,974,000 tennis balls.

It's not too difficult to know this, given the number of balls hit in an hour, the number of hours in a day, and when you know you've scarcely missed a day. But how many balls have to be hit before you can say, *"I am a tennis player!"* Millions of beginners hit thousands of balls and still remain beginners. The need for a better method of learning laid the seed for RHYTHMETONICS.

All those balls in forty years. Ten of those years were spent teaching tennis at a fashionable tennis club, where students paid a handsome fee for private instruction. At most clubs like ours, you will find high-powered lighting, expensive clay (or one of the rubberized surfaces), costly heating units for winter, elaborate air-conditioning for summer. So it's quite understandable why tennis lessons (indoors or out) are so expensive. But what do any of these things have to do with *learning* to play tennis? Teaching methods, not facilities, make you the tennis player—and proper teaching methods can best be employed at home.

There's a strange compulsion when you try to *learn* to play tennis on a tennis court. You feel like romping and running, jumping and stretching in your chase for the ball. But, to learn correctly, you don't run—you *pivot*; you don't stretch— you *reach*; and you don't jump—you *bend*! So I submit that you can learn to play tennis more correctly *in a closet* than on a tennis court (at least your strokes would be more compact). If it's big enough to turn in, to bend in, to reach in, and to swing your arm in, *any space can lend itself to learning*.

For years, on the court, I found myself pleading, "Why don't you copy me?" "Get that hip out of the way, like so, when you take that racquet back." "Flex those knees, like so, when you practice that Serve." "Copy me." Copy me!" But only after hours and hours, weeks and weeks, months and months— like a sculptor cutting at a piece of marble—could I chisel out the resemblance of a tennis player. *But I found the answer!*

Surely one's body cannot be expected to effectively move a ball, if it has not first learned to move itself!

It is difficult to learn the rudiments of a stroke when facing an onrushing ball. It is the ball's nature to be unyielding, and thought is too slow. When the ball short-circuits basic movement patterns, the result is imperfect practice (that can be, and often is, irreparable.) But there is no imperfect practice in exercise. The body of the most uncoordinated can become a dynamic force when paralysis from the ball is eliminated. *Rehearse the part before you play it.* Success is achieved by *correct repetition*, for the body needs to be *conditioned* more than taught.

You must move like a tennis player to be one; hence, RHYTHMETONICS. You won't have a ball to be mesmerized by—causing a late preparation, or none at all. Since *there is no ball*, you are not forced to hit it before you've learned how!

Like actors, tennis players do not allow the ball to upstage them but, rather, move to its rhythm. When you take the ball's rhythm, *you don't need the ball*—and you can learn to play tennis at home.

Classic movement patterns inherent in each tennis stroke adhere to the ball's rhythm. When these *movement patterns* are isolated from the stroke, and the *rhythm* is abstracted from the ball, you can exercise these patterns to the ball's rhythm. When you take the exercises out of the strokes and bring them into your living room, and practice them, your body will yield to the repetition and leave as its legacy the image of a champion. The living room favors the disciplines—the court the challenge. *You must learn this way!*

Practice is an attempt to make skill a habit. You can avoid imperfect practice in tennis by letting *perfect practice* begin. The RHYTHMETONICS exercise system will allow you to avoid passive reactions on the tennis court by developing active responses at home. It will teach you to *move to the ball's rhythm*. The exercises will internalize movement and condition reflexes. This is the foundation on which RHYTHMETONICS teaches.

I have not forgotten the feeling of being a beginner. That deficiency in muscle tone that leaves the body limp, that inability to coordinate one movement with another, that uncertain air. If exercise can circumvent this initial stage in learning— then why not circumvent it? Let exercise at home transcend that which is awkward, embarrassing and often counterproductive. *Let* RHYTHMETONICS *teach!*

Now, for the first time, through RHYTHMETONICS, tennis strokes can be exercised *at home, in a gymnasium, in a classroom—ANYWHERE!— without a ball or a tennis court.*

RHYTHMETONICS will revolutionize the teaching of tennis—*EVERYWHERE!*

Chapter 2

THE THEORY
OF RHYTHMETONICS

In the science of body movement, the greatest possible exercise, relating to sport, is that exercise which carries within it the same factors required for the final performance. RHYTHMETONICS zeros in on that principle.

The nervous system has a plasticity which, under stress, provides the ability to learn, to remember or to forget, and, with the appropriate stimuli, to condition. RHYTHMETONICS repetition *grooves*.

As you follow the RHYTHMETONICS exercises, you will proceed without the ball and discover the relationship between these exercises and the body language of tennis. The exercises, diagrammed to match the classic tennis strokes, teach "muscle memory." You will first learn the *rhythm* each stroke requires before stepping onto a tennis court. By constant repetition, only *positive* impulses will bombard your body, and the nervous system, not knowing the real from the unreal, will respond to the "ghost" of the ball.

The *body* determines a ball's movement. Body timing regulates it. Therefore, it is the body (*not* the ball) and the body's *anticipation* of hitting the ball that must be timed. By practicing separately the exercise movements into which each stroke is divided, you will condition reflexes and develop the appropriate body musculature for tennis. Each chapter is programmed to provide an easy, step-by-step method whereby you become the architect in a neuromuscular blueprint for tennis.

In following this revolutionary concept, every member of the family, each with his or her own particular flair, can learn to play tennis and enjoy the benefits of a healthy body—the natural way!

STEP I

Chapter 3
THE GRIP AND THE GAME

Around and around the hand goes—where it stops, nobody knows. Top players hit all around the racquet. Although champions may subscribe to a basic grip, they deviate from it as often as the ball demands, providing their bodies the flexibility required to meet the ball's challenge. Through subtle grip deviations, they can exact leverage where leverage is needed, apply power where power is due. They are well aware of their body's limitations and, by adjusting and readjusting, wield their racquets as if they were tools. As a painter turns a brush to effect a different touch, the champion, aware of the need for flexibility, through expert racquet handling, achieves it.

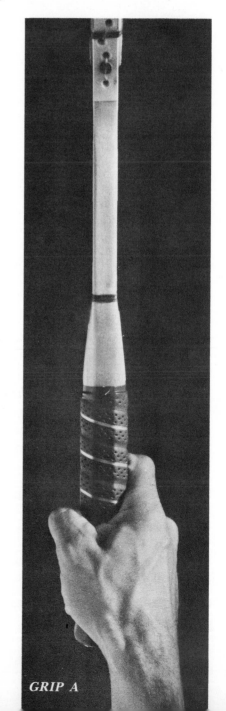

All too often these expediencies are lost to beginners. Frequently, beginners are provided "specific" grips designed more for accomplished players, whose bodies have long since learned to move and to react with the speed of a reflex.

There is no one grip that is perfect; and yet, how you hold your racquet will determine your style on the tennis court—even more, it will determine your ability *to effectively move*.

Beginners must be given guidelines that do not obstruct but, rather, adapt to expeditious movement. The hand should not be forced into clockwise and counter-clockwise turns: such grips are too inflexible. One should be given a grip that is most accessible to change, yet changes least.

GRIP A and *GRIP B* for RHYTHMETONICS are the most flexible grips in tennis. Their usage has produced some of the most colorful tennis the world has ever seen.

GRIP A: Your palm and wrist are *toward* the top surface of the racquet handle. The V between your thumb and forefinger is slightly left of center— there is space between your first and second fingers.

6

GRIP A

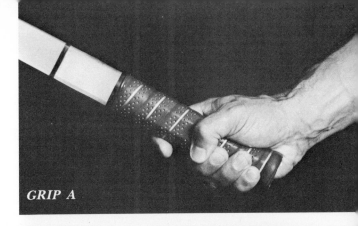

GRIP A

Your thumb and fingers are curled around the racquet. A slight angle is formed by your wrist and the racquet. (*GRIP A* is used for hitting the Forehand.)

When you determine that the ball is to your Backhand side, you must change from *GRIP A* to *GRIP B*. Relax *GRIP A*. Raise the racquet head slightly with the fingers of your left hand by pulling the edge of the racquet back toward your body. Take *GRIP B*.

GRIP B: Your palm and wrist are on the top surface of the racquet handle. The V has been pressed toward the left bevel of the racquet. Your thumb now extends further behind the racquet handle. (*GRIP B* is used for hitting the Serve, Backhand and Volley.)

Keep your grip firm until the end of the stroke. Tighten your grip on impact.

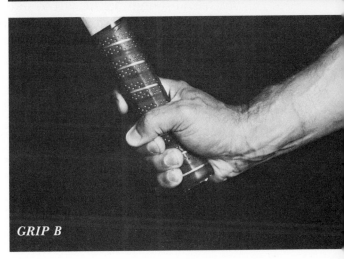

GRIP B

Chapter 4

THE LOW FOREHAND

A tennis ball has a special rhythm all its own when being hit or tossed to you. Time it.

TOSS . . . (2 seconds) . . . **BOUNCE** . . . (1 second) . . . **HIT!**

When you consider a stroke consists of three movements—a preparation, a backswing and a forward thrust—and when you learn to synchronize these movements with the *rhythm* of an approaching ball—on **TOSS** you prepare; on **BOUNCE** you get the racquet back; and on **HIT!** you reach out and swing at the ball—you begin to realize that tennis is, and should be, *an exercise in rhythm* and you have learned the key to good tennis.

Since the Forehand is the stroke most used in tennis, we'll begin with that.

NET →

BASELINE

Take *GRIP A* and the *READY STANCE*. **COPY ME.** Your feet are aligned and approximately 12 inches apart; your knees are slightly flexed. The fingers of your left hand are controlling the racquet at the throat.

THE LOW FOREHAND

TOSS

Gently *lift* your arm and elbow and, in the same smooth motion, *pivot* to the right on the ball of your left foot and the heel of your right. (These movements are done simultaneously.) The racquet does not go back as you pivot; it simply lifts. The fingers of your left hand are even with your left shoulder.

COPY ME. Your weight is resting comfortably on your right foot; your left heel is raised. The fingers of your left hand have tilted the racquet face inward slightly. (This is to help prevent your wrist from breaking back too soon.) Your right elbow and your left elbow are on an even plane. Your eyes are on the ball.

It is the total unawareness of this preparation movement that prevents beginners
from developing a smooth, rhythmic stroke.

THE LOW FOREHAND

Exercise 1

Having patterned the course your body must take, internalize this movement through exercise. The first exercise for THE LOW FOREHAND will be the **TOSS** movement. You'll simply move from the *READY STANCE* to the **TOSS** position and back again to *READY*.

Now from your *READY STANCE,* exercise this movement until you look like me.

COPY ME

TOSS

and back again to *READY* . . .

TOSS

and back again . . .

TOSS . . .

13

BOUNCE

From your **TOSS** position, *release* your fingers from the throat of the racquet. While holding your right shoulder in place, *slant* the edge of the racquet back toward your right shoulder as you *roll your wrist* around and downward, turning the face of the racquet until the strings are parallel with the front of your body. This will straighten your right arm and place your right elbow in front of and very close to your right hip. Simultaneously, pick your left foot up and *step* sideways toward the net, shifting your hips forward as you press your weight gradually onto the inside of the ball of your left foot. (Your step should be no wider than your shoulders.) The inward turn of your left shoulder will force your torso to coil to the right.

COPY ME. Your weight is resting firmly on your left foot. Your right knee is slanted inward. Your right arm is straight and perpendicular to the floor. Your right wrist is locked back.

The tighter you draw your body—the harder you will hit the ball.

THE LOW FOREHAND

Exercise 2

The second exercise for THE LOW FOREHAND will be the **BOUNCE** movement. You'll simply move from the **TOSS** position to the **BOUNCE** position and back again to **TOSS.**

Now from your **TOSS** position, exercise this movement until you look like me.

COPY ME

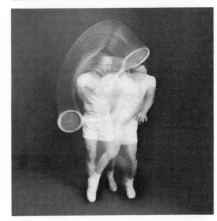

BOUNCE

and back again to **TOSS . . .**

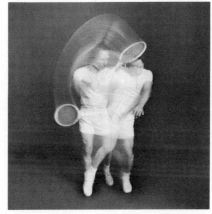

BOUNCE

and back again . . .

BOUNCE . . .

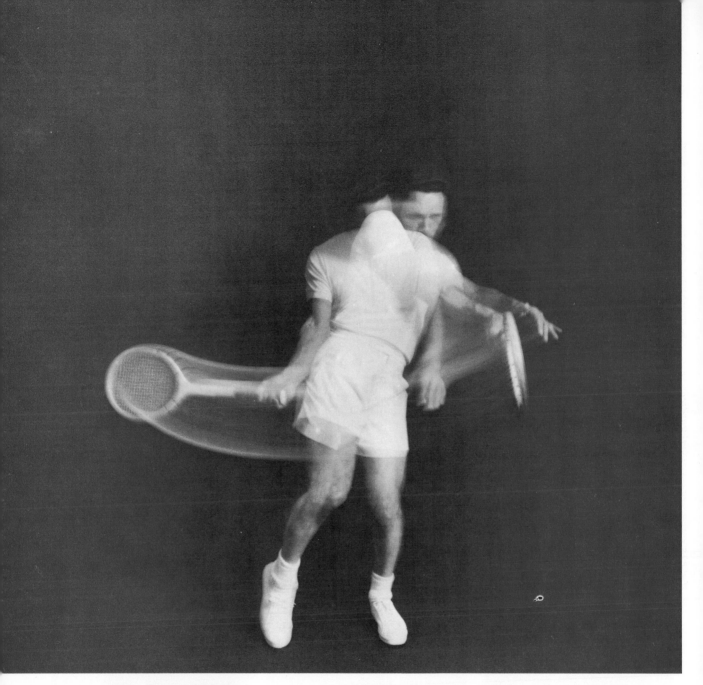

HIT!

From your **BOUNCE** position, *lock your wrist back*. *Stabilize* your left hip as you uncoil your torso. *Push* your right elbow forward with your shoulder, keeping it close to your body. *Swivel* your right foot until your toe points forward. *Keep your wrist firm*. (These movements are done simultaneously.)

COPY ME. Your right heel is raised. Your left arm is balancing your body. The racquet is out front toward the net.

Hand-eye coordination begins here!

At this point, brush the racquet strings up on the ball. . . .

The top of the racquet points *up* toward the ceiling. **COPY ME.**

THE LOW FOREHAND

Exercise 3

The final exercise for THE LOW FOREHAND will be the **HIT!** movement. You'll simply move from the **BOUNCE** position through the **HIT!** position as you add the *FOLLOW THROUGH*.

Now from your **BOUNCE** position, exercise this movement until you look like me.

COPY ME

and back again to **BOUNCE . . .**

and back again . . .

22

HIT!   and *FOLLOW THROUGH . . .*

HIT!   and *FOLLOW THROUGH . . .*

HIT!   and *FOLLOW THROUGH.*

When you combine the stroke's three movements and add its *FOLLOW THROUGH*, you've got . . .

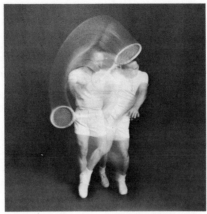

TOSS . . .   **BOUNCE . . .**   **HIT!**

and *FOLLOW THROUGH*.

THE LOW FOREHAND exemplifies the manner in which our tennis tattoos will be drawn. The goal is to reduce new movement patterns to the automatism of a reflex.

Once you develop confidence in practicing the stroke's movements, eliminate the pause at the end of the **BOUNCE** movement and you will create a more fluid LOW FOREHAND.

When you feel you've begun to internalize this classic tennis stroke, stand with your *left* side close to a wall. When you can successfully take your racquet back without touching the wall on your backswing and without hitting the wall on your *FOLLOW THROUGH*, then you'll know you are well on your way to developing the classic LOW FOREHAND stroke. Through exercise, you'll master it.

Chapter 5

THE LOW BACKHAND

Before we get into stroke production, I think we should first deal with the notion that the Backhand is more difficult than the Forehand. Is it real, or imaginary? Tennis teachers tell us the Backhand is the more natural stroke and, of course, this is true. But this truth does little to ease the frustration in millions of beginning tennis players who, in spite of the sense of it, find the Backhand more difficult. Imaginary? Surely not to those who practice it for hours and then pose the question, "If the Backhand's more *natural,* why am I not hitting it?"

RHYTHMETONICS teaches that the trauma caused by an onrushing ball short-circuits basic movement patterns and denies the body the experience necessary to develop the appropriate musculature for achievement. The Backhand can be one of the most beautiful strokes in tennis, perhaps because *it is a more natural stroke.* The arm is flung out and away from the body with an "inside-out" movement, and unlike the Forehand where the elbow is somewhat restricted (the body being in the elbow's way), the arm has freedom of movement. When given a **TOSS** . . . **BOUNCE** . . . **HIT!** rhythm the Backhand can be as graceful as ballet. A rhythm that accentuates artful movement is evident in every classic tennis stroke. So signals that *excite* reflexes and exercises that *condition* them can be a *short-cut* to *perfection.*

NET

BASELINE

Take *GRIP B* and the *READY STANCE*. The *READY STANCE* for THE LOW BACKHAND is the same as that for THE LOW FOREHAND. **COPY ME.**

THE LOW BACKHAND

TOSS

Gently *lift* your arm and elbow and, in the same smooth motion, *pivot* to the left on the ball of your right foot and the heel of your left. (These movements are done simultaneously.) The racquet does not go back as you pivot; it simply lifts. Your left elbow is even with your left hip.

COPY ME. Your weight is resting comfortably on your left foot; your right heel is raised. The fingers of your left hand are controlling the racquet face. Your right elbow is lower than your left elbow. The edge of the racquet is facing toward you. Your eyes are on the ball.

You are now in a prepared position awaiting the bounce of the ball.

THE LOW BACKHAND

Exercise 1

The first exercise for THE LOW BACKHAND will be the **TOSS** movement. You'll simply move from the *READY STANCE* to the **TOSS** position and back again to *READY*.

Now from your *READY STANCE*, exercise this movement until you look like me.

COPY ME

TOSS

and back again to *READY* . . .

TOSS

and back again . . .

TOSS . . .

31

BOUNCE

From your **TOSS** position, *slant* the edge of the racquet toward your left shoulder as you *roll your wrist* around and downward, turning the face of the racquet until the strings are parallel with the front of your body. This will straighten your right arm and place your right elbow in front of and very close to your right hip. Simultaneously, pick your right foot up and *step* sideways toward the net, shifting your hips forward as you press your weight gradually onto the inside of the ball of your right foot. (Your step should be no wider than your shoulders.) The inward turn of your right shoulder will force your torso to coil to the left.

COPY ME. Your weight is resting firmly on your right foot. Your left knee is slanted inward. Your right arm is straight and perpendicular to the floor. Your right wrist is locked back. The fingers of your left hand are controlling the racquet face at its throat and your left elbow is behind your back.

The tightness you feel in your right hip is a signal that your balance is stable.

THE LOW BACKHAND

Exercise 2

The second exercise for THE LOW BACKHAND will be the **BOUNCE** movement. You'll simply move from the **TOSS** position to the **BOUNCE** position and back again to **TOSS.**

Now from your **TOSS** position, exercise this movement until you look like me.

COPY ME

BOUNCE

and back again to **TOSS . . .**

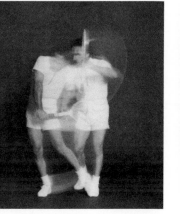

BOUNCE

and back again . . .

BOUNCE . . .

HIT!

From your **BOUNCE** position, *release* the fingers of your left hand from the throat of the racquet. Keep your right wrist locked back. *Stabilize* your right hip as you uncoil your torso. *Hold* your left shoulder back. *Pull* your right arm with your right shoulder from inside out. *Swivel* your left foot until your toe points forward. (These movements are done simultaneously.)

COPY ME. Your left heel is raised. Your left arm (in back of you) balances your body. The racquet is out front toward the net. Your eyes are on the ball.

Hand-eye coordination begins here!

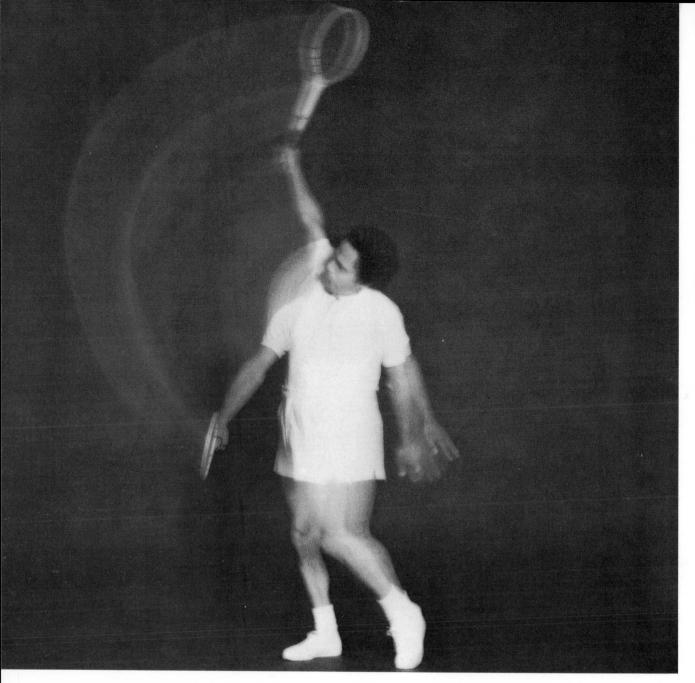

At this point the back of your right hand gives way to the racquet head. . . .

The small of your back *tightens;* your chest *expands;* the racquet finishes high above your head.
COPY ME.

THE LOW BACKHAND

Exercise 3

The final exercise for THE LOW BACKHAND will be the **HIT!** movement. You'll simply move from the **BOUNCE** position through the **HIT!** position as you add the *FOLLOW THROUGH*.

Now from your **BOUNCE** position, exercise this movement until you look like me.

COPY ME

and back again to **BOUNCE . . .**

and back again . . .

HIT!   and *FOLLOW THROUGH . . .*

HIT!   and *FOLLOW THROUGH . . .*

HIT!   and *FOLLOW THROUGH.*

When you combine the stroke's three movements and add its *FOLLOW THROUGH*, you've got . . .

TOSS . . .   **BOUNCE . . .**   **HIT!**

and *FOLLOW THROUGH*.

You'll begin to feel the sense of it as you practice this classic tennis stroke. Each time you practice an exercise, it will become more graceful until the last vestige of awkward and uncoordinated movement is gone.

When you feel you've begun to internalize this classic tennis stroke, stand with your *right* side close to a wall. When you can successfully take your racquet back without touching the wall on your backswing and without hitting the wall on your *FOLLOW THROUGH* then you'll know you are well on your way to developing the classic LOW BACKHAND stroke. Through exercise, you'll master it.

Chapter 6

RISING BALLS

There are falling balls (THE LOW FOREHAND and THE LOW BACKHAND) and there are rising balls (THE HIGH FOREHAND and THE HIGH BACKHAND) and the degree to which your body adjusts to their differences is the measure by which you can truly be called *a tennis player*.

It is possible to interpret perfect ground strokes (the Forehand and the Backhand) but still miss the ball, whenever the mind cannot compute nor the body measure the ball's errant ways. "Out of sync" are the body coordinates that must move with the automatism of a reflex but instead are at variance with every new turn of the ball. The fact that a ball never comes across the net twice the same way can be disabling to a beginner. It is the ball's up and down movement that tends to make the beginner miss.

When a ball is hit or tossed to you, in its flight, it rises, reaches its crest and then falls. The ball's bounce and your distance from it will determine whether the ball will be rising or falling when you hit it.

Your preparation **(TOSS)** position adapts to both falling and rising balls. It enables you to adjust the racquet head to the ball's bounce. You either *roll your wrist downward* to hit the falling ball or *lock your wrist back* for the rising ball.

To prepare by taking the racquet straight back (as many beginners do) is better than not getting the racquet back at all, but this is often incompatible with hitting falling and rising balls. If you must dig for the falling ball and lunge for the rising ball, then your game may be more acrobatics than tennis.

Take *GRIP A*. The movement from the *READY STANCE* to the preparation **(TOSS)** position for THE HIGH FOREHAND is the same as that for THE LOW FOREHAND.   **COPY ME.**

THE HIGH FOREHAND

BOUNCE

From your **TOSS** position, *release* your fingers from the throat of the racquet. While holding your right shoulder in place, *turn* the inside strings of the racquet *outward* toward the net. As you *pull* your upper arm in toward your body, *straighten your elbow* and *lock your wrist back*. This will force your shoulder to lift and to press close to your right ear. Simultaneously, pick your left foot up and with your left leg straight, *step diagonally* toward the net *slanting your left foot inward* as you step. The inward turn of your left shoulder will force your torso to coil to the right.

COPY ME. Your weight is resting firmly on your straight left leg. Your right heel is raised. Your right knee is tight. Your wrist is locked back. The racquet head is slanting up. Your right shoulder is pressed close to your ear.

Your body pulls as in a tug of war—body balance against leverage.

THE HIGH FOREHAND

Exercise 1

The first exercise for THE HIGH FOREHAND will be the **BOUNCE** movement. You'll simply move from the **TOSS** position to the **BOUNCE** position and back again to **TOSS.**

Now from your **TOSS** position, exercise this movement until you look like me.

COPY ME

BOUNCE

and back again to **TOSS** . . .

BOUNCE

and back again . . .

BOUNCE . . .

HIT!

From your **BOUNCE** position, keep your wrist *locked back* and *stabilize* your left hip as you uncoil your torso. *Push* your right elbow forward with your shoulder, keeping it close to your body. *Swivel* your right foot until your toe points forward. *Keep your wrist firm.* (These movements are done simultaneously.)

COPY ME. Your right heel is raised. Your left arm is balancing your body. The racquet face is parallel to the net. Your eyes are on the ball.

More from the pace of the ball than from the force of the body can be the rising ball's sting.

At this point, a *firm wrist* carries the racquet through the ball. . . .

The racquet finishes high above your head. **COPY ME.**

THE HIGH FOREHAND

Exercise 2

The second and final exercise for THE HIGH FOREHAND will be the **HIT!** movement. You'll simply move from the **BOUNCE** position through the **HIT!** position as you add the *FOLLOW THROUGH*.

Now from your **BOUNCE** position, exercise this movement until you look like me.

COPY ME

and back again to **BOUNCE . . .**

and back again . . .

54

HIT! and *FOLLOW THROUGH . . .*

HIT! and *FOLLOW THROUGH . . .*

 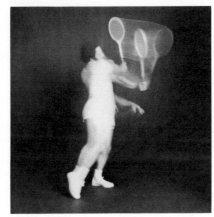 

HIT! and *FOLLOW THROUGH.*

When you combine the stroke's three movements and add its *FOLLOW THROUGH*, you've got . . .

TOSS . . .   **BOUNCE . . .**   **HIT!**

and *FOLLOW THROUGH*.

Exercise THE HIGH FOREHAND—be as exact as you can—until the sinews in your muscles remember.

Take *GRIP B*. The movement from the *READY STANCE* to the preparation **(TOSS)** position for THE HIGH BACKHAND is the same as that for THE LOW BACK-HAND. **COPY ME.**

THE HIGH BACKHAND

BOUNCE

From your **TOSS** position, hold your right shoulder in place and *tilt* the face of the racquet back with the fingers of your left hand. *Straighten your right arm*. Simultaneously, pick your right foot up and with your right leg straight *step diagonally* toward the net—*slanting your right foot inward* as you step. While stepping, *pull* your straight right arm across your upper torso. The inward turn of your right shoulder will force your torso to coil to the left.

COPY ME. Your weight is resting firmly on your straight right leg. Your left heel is raised. Your left knee is tight. Your fingers on the throat of the racquet are sustaining your arm's tension, as the pull of your right shoulder slants the inside edge of the racquet toward your body. Your wrist is locked back. The racquet head is slanting up.

The tightness you feel in your right shoulder is a body tension that can be likened to a slingshot just before it snaps.

THE HIGH BACKHAND

Exercise 1

The first exercise for THE HIGH BACKHAND will be the **BOUNCE** movement. You'll simply move from the **TOSS** position to the **BOUNCE** position and back again to **TOSS.**

Now from your **TOSS** position, exercise this movement until you look like me.

COPY ME

BOUNCE

and back again to **TOSS . . .**

BOUNCE

and back again . . .

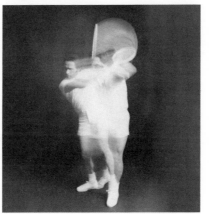

BOUNCE . . .

61

HIT!

From your **BOUNCE** position, *release* the fingers of your left hand from the throat of the racquet. *Keep your right wrist firm. Stabilize* your right hip as you uncoil your torso. *Hold* your left shoulder back. *Pull* your right arm with your right shoulder from inside out. *Swivel* your left foot until your toe points forward. (These movements are done simultaneously.)

COPY ME.   Your left heel is raised. Your left arm is behind your body and balancing it. The racquet face is parallel to the net. Your eyes are on the ball.

The ball seems to play itself as the pace from its bounce presses up on the strings of the racquet, and then, as if attacking the opponent with his own force, reverses itself.

At this point, a *firm wrist* carries the racquet through the ball. . . .

The racquet finishes high above your head. **COPY ME.**

THE HIGH
BACKHAND

Exercise 2

The second and final exercise for *THE HIGH BACKHAND* will be the **HIT!** movement. You'll simply move from the **BOUNCE** position through the **HIT!** position as you add the *FOLLOW THROUGH*.

Now from your **BOUNCE** position, exercise this movement until you look like me.

COPY ME

and back again to **BOUNCE . . .**

and back again . . .

HIT! and *FOLLOW THROUGH . . .*

HIT! and *FOLLOW THROUGH . . .*

HIT! and *FOLLOW THROUGH.*

When you combine the stroke's three movements and add its *FOLLOW THROUGH,* you've got . . .

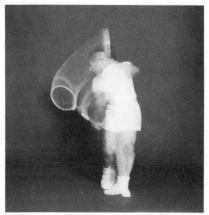  

TOSS . . . **BOUNCE . . .** **HIT!**
and *FOLLOW THROUGH.*

You have just exercised my favorite stroke. To me, THE HIGH BACKHAND is the only stroke that allows the body to unleash its *total power* and still maintain a graceful balance. It is not just hitting the ball that intrigues me so. It is the esthetics in the stroke's preparation. The artful way in which the body must turn itself out of the arm's way as it moves on a rising ball. The "getting there" just as the ball, from its bounce, rises above the level of the net and then, the anticipation of hitting it. As you look over your shoulder, as all top players do, there is a simple purity: the ball . . . the net . . . and the baseline.

Exercise THE HIGH BACKHAND until the movements become fixed, until the sinews in your muscles remember.

The difference between *learning* to play tennis and really playing is the **BOUNCE** of the ball—and *time*. These are the determinants by which the ball will either be rising or falling. If the position of the racquet head is to relate properly to the **BOUNCE** of the ball, then the body must be quick to respond.

Chart the ball's **BOUNCE** through exercise, and relate the **BOUNCE** of the ball to time. You'll simply move from the **TOSS** position to the **BOUNCE** positions for THE HIGH and LOW FOREHAND . . . and back again to **TOSS**.

THE FOREHAND

FALLING BALL
(LOW FOREHAND)

RISING BALL
(HIGH FOREHAND)

COPY ME

BOUNCE . . . and back to **TOSS**

BOUNCE

and back again . . .

BOUNCE . . .and back to **TOSS**

BOUNCE

and back again . . .

BOUNCE . . . and back to **TOSS**

BOUNCE.

And repeat this exercise for the Backhand. Now from your **TOSS** position, exercise these movements until you look like me.

THE BACKHAND

FALLING BALL (LOW BACKHAND)	RISING BALL (HIGH BACKHAND)

 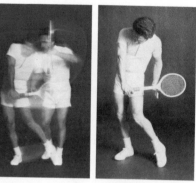  

COPY ME   *BOUNCE* . . . and back to **TOSS**   **BOUNCE**

and back again . . .   *BOUNCE* . . . and back to **TOSS**   **BOUNCE**

and back again . . .   *BOUNCE* . . . and back to **TOSS**   **BOUNCE.**

Exercise the ground strokes until they become internalized and hitting rising balls or falling balls becomes automatic. When advanced tennis begins to evolve from the rudiments, you need not wait to be daring, for *the ground strokes are yours*. Exercise them.

70

Chapter 7
THE SERVE

No stroke in tennis has suffered more the oversimplification syndrome than the Serve. "Pitch like a pitcher!" "Make a tossed ball stand still—and you've got yourself a Serve." How frustrating it is for beginners when they find it's easier said than done. No stroke in tennis is easy, but no stroke need be made arduous through complicated theorem.

It's enough to know that the object in hitting a Serve is to create maximum force on the tennis ball, and that this is done through sequential muscle contraction— first the **COIL,** then the **UNCOIL,** then the **SNAP!** But to be ladened with the twistings and extensions that occur in the classic tennis Serve (while facing a ball ruthlessly hostile to an untrained body) can clutter thought and paralyze movement, and render beginners helpless. Little wonder, that the inexperienced lose their bout with the ball and the classic tennis Serve eludes them.

Preparation is key to developing a proper Serve. If the preparation motion is interfered with by the toss of the ball, then you have a faulty preparation and nothing can properly follow. So it might be very simple to practice tossing up balls, but if your body has not *first* learned the Serve's preparation movement, if it must adjust to the ball's toss, rather than *the toss to the coiled body,* then the body's natural rotation back into the ball will be limited.

In baseball you know the ball is to come over the plate, but the plate and the ball itself would be meaningless were the body not coiled to hit it. Does it not follow— if the toss of the ball causes imperfect practice, then *the ball should go?*

Nothing stands in your way now that the "antagonist" is gone. Simply piece together this classic tennis Serve and, *through exercise,* master it.

Prepare to do your first exercise for the Serve without the racquet.

Rise up on your toes for three seconds, then relax.

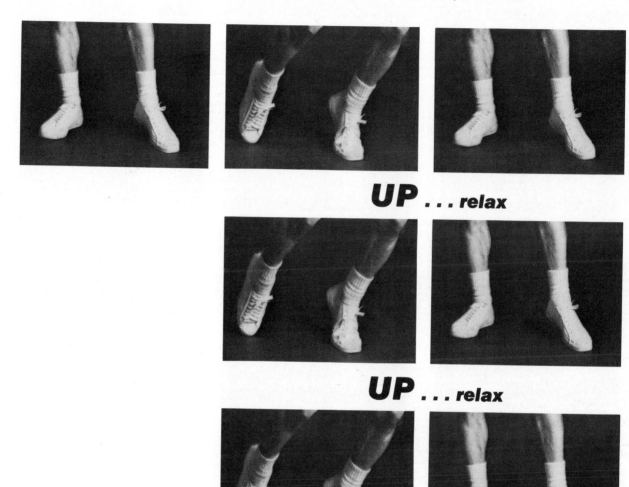

UP . . . **relax**

UP . . . **relax**

UP . . . **relax**

Now this time while up on your toes, *bend your torso back.* You'll find that this will flex your knees a bit.

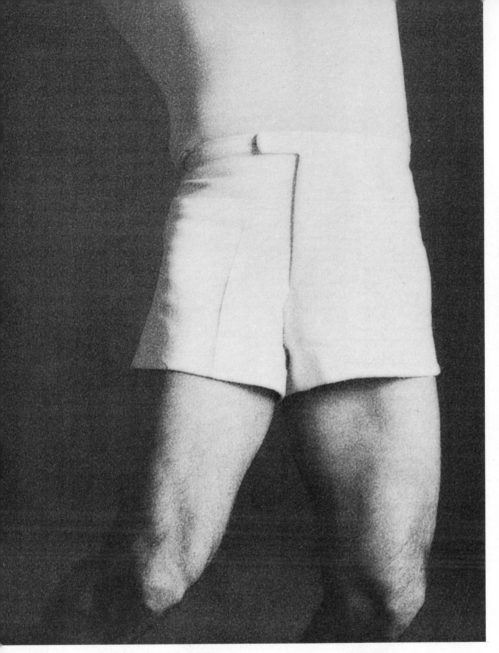

UP . . . relax   UP . . . relax   UP . . . relax

Now you may have toddled a bit, but somewhere between the arched back and the flexed knees *there is a balancing point*. Through *practice*, you'll find it . . . and with it, *a body balance* that is essential to the Serve's preparation movement.

Now this time, gently *lift your left arm* straight up into the air. The *palm* of your hand will be facing the ceiling. As your right shoulder lowers, you'll feel yourself *coil slightly to the right as your weight transfers itself*, through your hips, onto the ball of your left foot.

UP . . . relax   UP . . . relax   UP . . . relax

Now this time, as you *lift* your left arm, *slowly pull* your right arm back and up. Your right elbow should be *level* with your right shoulder, your fist *close* to your head, and the *back* of your right hand facing the ceiling.

UP . . . **relax**   **UP** . . . **relax**   **UP** . . . **relax**

Almost without thought, you've exercised your body in a movement known only to the champions—and to the well-tutored.

NET →

Now, with the racquet, take *GRIP B* and the Serve's *READY STANCE*. **COPY ME.** Your body is leaning back toward your right foot and your weight is resting on it. Your left foot is at a *45° angle* to it. The fingers of your left hand are cradling the racquet at the throat and are directly above your left toe out in front of your body. Your right wrist is low. Your glance is toward the net.

THE SERVE

COIL

Release the fingers of your left hand from the throat of the racquet. *Lower* the racquet head to the level of your right knee. *Lower* your left hand slightly. *Assume* your final **UP** position, previously acquired without the racquet. (These movements are done simultaneously.)

COPY ME. Your heels are *raised*. Your knees are *flexed*. Your torso is *coiled* to the right. Your right forearm and wrist are in a *snapping* position. Your eyes are on the ball. (When on the court, you will toss the ball from the fingers of your left hand *after* your body's coil.)

Poised in a static contraction, your body now awaits its second movement.

THE SERVE

Exercise 1

The first exercise for THE SERVE will be the **COIL** movement. You'll simply move from the Serve's *READY STANCE* to the **COIL** position and back again to *READY*.

Now from your *READY STANCE*, exercise this movement until you look like me.

COPY ME

COIL

and back again to *READY* . . .

COIL

and back again . . .

COIL . . .

UNCOIL

From your **COIL** *position, pull your left arm downward. Turn* your right shoulder and hip toward the net as you *uncoil* your torso. *Swivel* your right foot until your toe points forward. *Lock* your right forearm and wrist back. (These movements are done simultaneously.) Care must be taken that your left hip *stabilize* your body as your right knee and elbow *snap* to the front.

COPY ME.   Your right heel is *raised*. The top of your torso is *turned* toward the net. The edge of the racquet is below your right shoulder blade. Your left arm and right elbow *pull against each other. Your body is taut.*

Breathing stops. You're in a strong contraction—the stronger the contraction, the more powerful the stroke.

THE SERVE

The second exercise for THE SERVE will be the **UNCOIL** movement. You'll simply move from the **COIL** position to the **UNCOIL** position and back again to **COIL.**

Now from your **COIL** position, exercise this movement until you look like me.

COPY ME

UNCOIL

and back again to **COIL...**

UNCOIL

and back again . . .

UNCOIL...

SNAP!

Rise even higher on the ball of your left foot. *Swing* your right forearm up. *Reach up* with your right shoulder and *lift* your right hip. *Straighten* your right leg. (These movements are done simultaneously.) Do not be content with just swinging down on the ball. This limits the Serve's potential. Your forearm swings *up* from beneath the tossed ball; the *snap* of your wrist will bring the ball down.

COPY ME. Your entire right side is *reaching up*. Your left hip is *stable*.

As your body uncoils from beneath the tossed ball—reach up for the peak of your power.

At this point, your natural left-to-right wrist *snap* explodes the racquet into the ball. . . .

Care must be taken that your left hip *continue to stabilize* your body as you *lift* your straight right leg into the court. **COPY ME.**

THE SERVE

Exercise 3

The final exercise for THE SERVE will be the **SNAP!** movement. You'll simply move from the **UNCOIL** position through the **SNAP!** position, as you add the *FOLLOW THROUGH*.

Now from your **UNCOIL** position, exercise this movement until you look like me.

COPY ME

and back again to **UNCOIL . . .**

and back again . . .

SNAP!   and *FOLLOW THROUGH . . .*

SNAP!   and *FOLLOW THROUGH . . .*

SNAP!   and *FOLLOW THROUGH.*

When you combine the stroke's three movements and add its *FOLLOW THROUGH,* you've got . . .

COIL . . . **UNCOIL . . .** **SNAP!**

and *FOLLOW THROUGH*

Now you can begin to take on *the antagonist,* assured in the knowledge that your bout with the ball will be won.

Chapter 8

THE VOLLEY

Pretend I am tossing you a ball. Now—with one hand—*catch it*! *If your arm is out front and your hand is "cocked" up,* you have just learned your motion for the Volley.

A Volley is a backswing taken in front of the body. More attitude than movement, more impact than stroke, it is a force repelled. Without beginning—and without end— it is the *middle* of a stroke. It is difficult for beginners to understand the efficiency of the Volley until their bodies have been trained to repel the ball's imposing force and exercised in the proper leverage to attack it. (*A static contraction must repel the ball's force and body finesse must direct it.*)

More *reflex* than thought is the demand of time, for the ball does not bounce in the Volley. Conditioned reflexes create active responses and the ball goes back over the net. Just as a bullfighter taunts a bull—close, but not too close— the Volley is a *measured movement.* While subtle body twists adjust to the ball, footwork steals the show.

Like standing on a clock,
you "measure" your movement and move in a framework of time.

Take *GRIP B* and the *READY STANCE*. The *READY STANCE* for the Volley is the same as that for the Forehand and for the Backhand. **COPY ME.**

THE VOLLEY

THE FOREHAND VOLLEY

Without a backsbing, *push* your elbow out in front of your body and *lock* your wrist back placing the racquet face in the path of the ball. Care must be taken when you step on the clock that *your right leg stabilize the right side of your body as your left shoulder turns inward . . .*

6

THE BACKHAND VOLLEY

and that *your left leg stabilize the left side of your body as your right shoulder turns inward*—or your body will lose its contraction, and the clock will lose time.

BLOCKING

GRIP B adapts best to the Volley. Its flexibility allows your wrist to roll and gives your elbow room

Now exercise the Volley. Use my footsteps as your guide.

You'll simply move from the *READY STANCE* to the Volley's **HIT!** position and back again to *READY*.

Now from your *READY STANCE, do it*!

THE FOREHAND VOLLEY

9 o'clock . . .   10 o'clock . . .
11 o'clock . . .   12 o'clock . . .
1 o'clock . . .   2 o'clock . . .
3 .

There must be no lost motion to move the Volley out of its time frame as you *turn* your torso *clockwise*

to reach out in front of your body on **HIT!** to *block* the ball, or *prod* it.

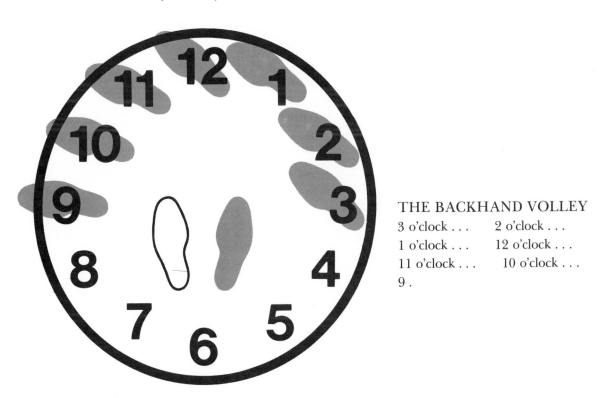

THE BACKHAND VOLLEY

3 o'clock . . .   2 o'clock . . .
1 o'clock . . .   12 o'clock . . .
11 o'clock . . .   10 o'clock . . .
9 .

and *counterclockwise* easing around toward the inside of the ball, like a matador parrying a bull.

97

Exercise the Volley again and as you practice its footwork, mark the flight of the ball by time.

Start with the Forehand Volley and alternate to the Backhand Volley. Then reverse from the Backhand to the Forehand Volley as on the following page.

Now from your *READY STANCE, do it*!

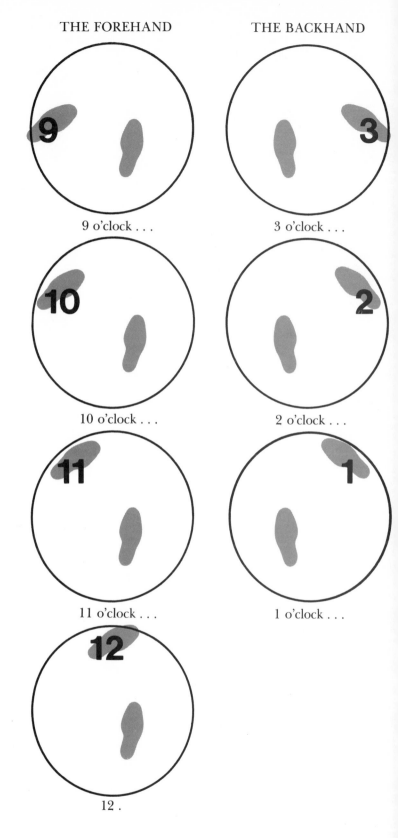

THE FOREHAND

THE BACKHAND

9 o'clock . . .

3 o'clock . . .

10 o'clock . . .

2 o'clock . . .

11 o'clock . . .

1 o'clock . . .

12 .

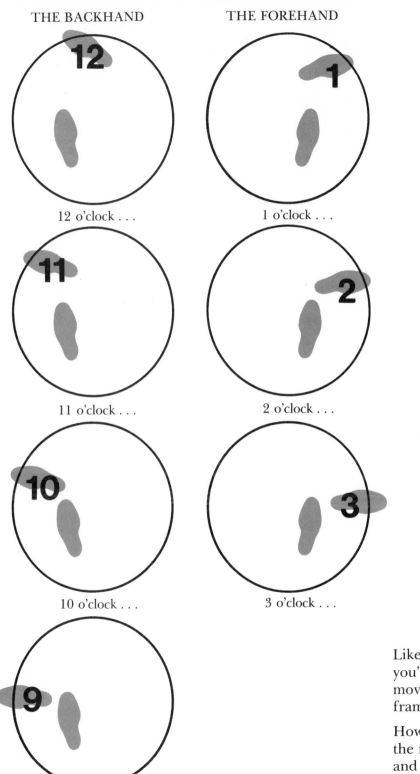

THE BACKHAND   THE FOREHAND

12 o'clock . . .

1 o'clock . . .

11 o'clock . . .

2 o'clock . . .

10 o'clock . . .

3 o'clock . . .

9 .

Like standing on a clock you've measured your movement and moved in a framework of time.

How else can you guard the net, attack the ball, and make an opponent's force your own?

99

Chapter 9

THE BEND IN THE STROKE

The ground strokes are the source from which auxiliary strokes develop. Auxiliary-stroke precisions cannot be attained until basic movement patterns have been set. It is a neuromuscular certainty that fine movements must develop from gross movements. There can be no finesse until the body has been sufficiently "honed" to produce the fineness of a touch.

The slices, the lobs, the drop shots are simply arrangements that the ground strokes have made with the racquet—with the slice it is turned, for the lob it is opened, with the drop shot the racquet is loosened. These strokes are a "play" on the ball, a touch of class; when you acquire the "feel" for the strokes, you become their master.

Slices, lobs and drop shots are bends in the stroke that color the game and express a personality often hidden from oneself. The cautious may slice. The clever may lob. The devil will "feather" a drop shot.

You also reveal yourself by the manner in which you hit the overhead. You either hit the ball hard and win the point or pamper it and play on. By exercising the overhead (the Serve's **UNCOIL** and **SNAP!**) you will develop muscle strength. (The shoulder will provide power for the "whip" of the forearm and force to the hammer-like fist.) In no way is the overhead subordinate to the Serve. It is equal in power. When you shorten the time span between the **UNCOIL** and **SNAP!** the power in the overhead inrreases.

The Slice: The longer a ball remains on the strings of the racquet, the more control you have over the ball—occasionally "spin off" a slice.

The cautious may *slice* . . .

The Lob: Used when your opponent is at the net or when you are in a defensive position—occasionally "push up" a lob deep to your opponent's backcourt.

the clever may *lob* . . .

The Drop Shot: Used when your opponent is deep in the backcourt and you are positioned in the area of your forecourt or in toward the net—sometimes "feather" a drop shot.

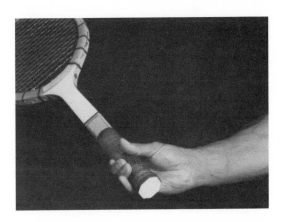

the devil will "feather" a *drop shot.*

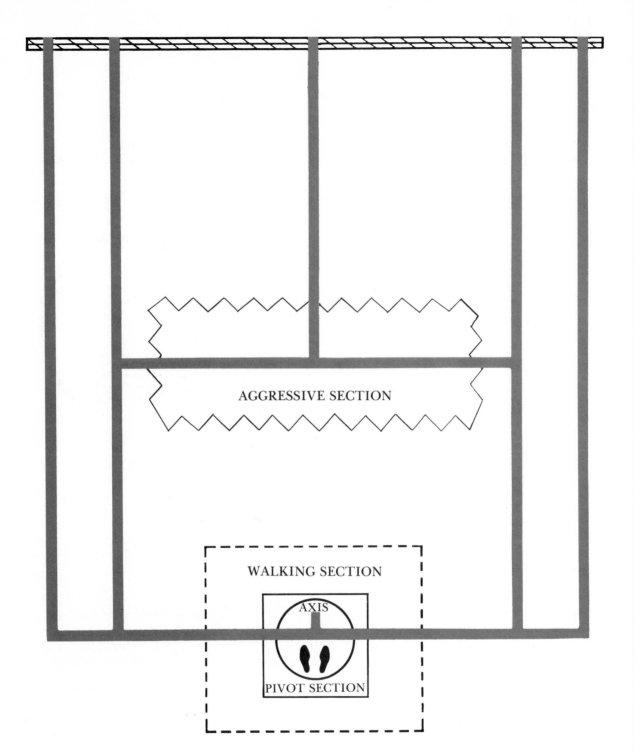

Chapter 10
AT HOME ON THE COURT

Your first priority after developing your strokes is to learn to move on the court. At left is a diagram of your side of the court showing the *AXIS* and the court's vital sections. Practice using the court's sections in your living room. Learn to use the court to your advantage—AT HOME.

THE AXIS

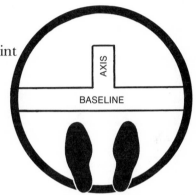

The *AXIS* at the center of the baseline is the focal point around which tennis players move on the court. When you use it as a constant point of reference, you can more easily judge what kinds of steps (short or long), and how many, to take (usually three) to reach any ball that comes within the area of the baseline. After completing a stroke in the vicinity of the *AXIS*, you must return to it, straddle it, and assume the *READY STANCE*.

THE PIVOT SECTION

A *PIVOT* is a step that *prepares* to turn your shoulder toward the ball. The *PIVOT* gives pause to your movement. From its stance you can manipulate time. Whether you are standing, walking or running, the last position of the *PIVOT* will be your final stance before the ball bounces (unless you are pulled totally out of position).

Your "body clock" starts ticking as you step toward the net from your **TOSS** position and your weight presses *gradually* onto the inside of the ball of your front foot, *constraining body tension until the ball has reached its "hitting area."* Your body must synchronize to the ball's rhythm for it is your body's *anticipation* of hitting the ball that is timed.

Establish a mental AXIS in your living room. Take your *READY STANCE*, and straddle it.

Remember as you move through each *PIVOT* to complete your **TOSS . . . BOUNCE . . . HIT!** movements with your racquet, add your *FOLLOW THROUGH*, then return to the *AXIS* and resume your *READY STANCE*.

Practice these *PIVOTS* and move to the ball's rhythm.

THE FOREHAND	THE BACKHAND

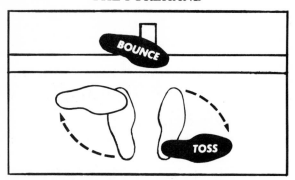 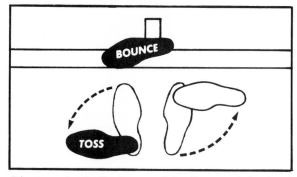

Pivot on the ball of your left foot and the heel of your right foot. Then *step sideways* toward the net with your left foot gradually transferring your weight onto it.

Pivot on the ball of your right foot and the heel of your left foot. Then *step sideways* toward the net with your right foot gradually transferring your weight onto it.

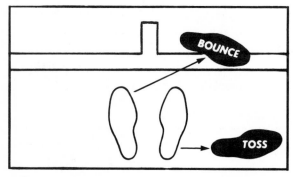 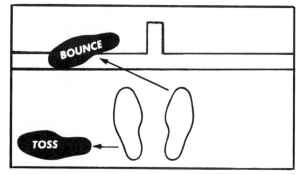

When a ball is a step away, *step* with your right foot. Then, *step sideways* toward the net with your left foot gradually transferring your weight onto it.

When a ball is a step away, *step* with your left foot. Then, *step sideways* toward the net with your right foot gradually transferring your weight onto it.

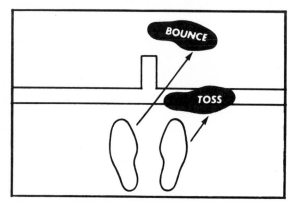 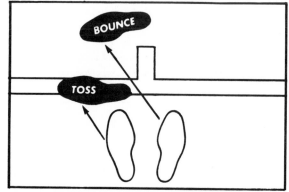

When a ball is a step short, *step sideways* toward it with your right foot. Then, *step sideways* toward the net with your left foot gradually transferring your weight onto it.

When a ball is a step short, *step sideways* toward it with your left foot. Then, *step sideways* toward the net with your right foot gradually transferring your weight onto it.

THE FOREHAND

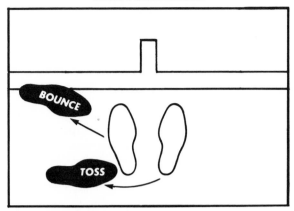

When a ball comes directly toward your body, *step* behind and around your left foot onto the ball of your right foot. As you lower your right heel, *step sideways* toward the net with your left foot gradually transferring your weight onto it.

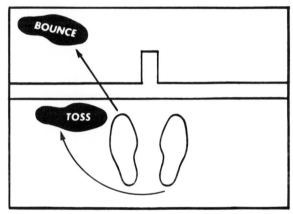

When a ball comes directly toward your body and is a step short, *step* behind and completely around to the front of your left foot onto the ball of your right foot. As you lower your right heel, *step sideways* toward the net with your left foot gradually transferring your weight onto it.

THE BACKHAND

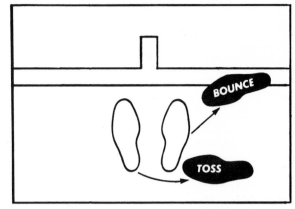

When a ball comes directly toward your body, *step* behind and around your right foot onto the ball of your left foot. As you lower your left heel, *step sideways* toward the net with your right foot gradually transferring your weight onto it.

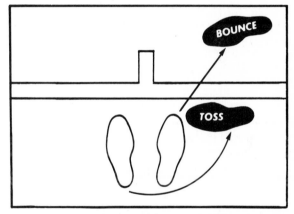

When a ball comes directly toward your body and is a step short, *step* behind and completely around to the front of your right foot onto the ball of your left foot. As you lower your left heel, *step sideways* toward the net with your right foot gradually transferring your weight onto it.

THE WALKING SECTION

When a ball's bounce carries it to within the area of the backcourt (out of reach of the *PIVOT SECTION*), it will be either a little short of the baseline, or a little long. In such cases, do not overreact by running in the court's *WALKING SECTION*.

Practice these steps in your living room. *Remember* to execute your **TOSS . . . BOUNCE . . . HIT!** movements and upon completion of your *FOLLOW THROUGH*, return to the *AXIS*.

THE FOREHAND

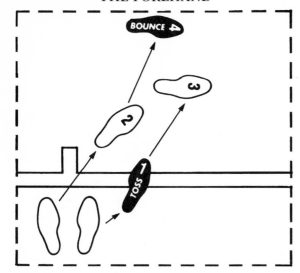

When a ball comes short to the Forehand, *step* toward the ball with your right foot and then with your left foot. Pick your right foot up and *step sideways* toward the ball. Then, *step sideways* toward the net with your left foot gradually transferring your weight onto it.

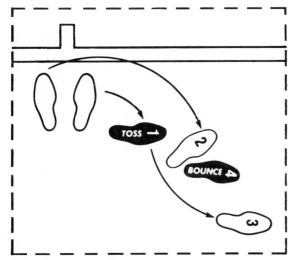

When a ball comes deep to the Forehand, *step diagonally* with your right foot away from the net. With your left foot, *step around* the front of your right foot and behind it. Pick your right foot up and place it in line with the oncoming ball. Then *step sideways* toward the net with your left foot gradually transferring your weight onto it.

The rest of the court is for running.

THE BACKHAND

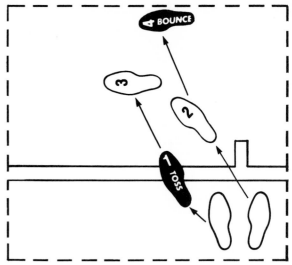

When a ball comes short to the Backhand, *step* toward the ball with your left foot and then with your right foot. Pick your left foot up and *step sideways* toward the ball. Then, *step sideways* toward the net with your right foot gradually transferring your weight onto it.

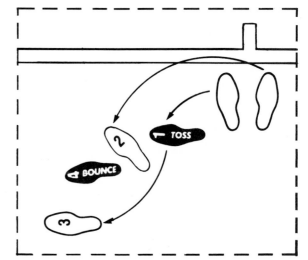

When a ball comes deep to the Backhand, *step diagonally* with your left foot away from the net. With your right foot, *step around* the front of your left foot and behind it. Pick your left foot up and place it in line with the oncoming ball. Then, *step sideways* toward the net with your right foot gradually transferring your weight onto it.

THE AGGRESSIVE SECTION

The "killer" instinct required in the *AGGRESSIVE SECTION* compels you to *attack* the ball while it is rising. It is not necessary to practice running to the *AGGRESSIVE SECTION* while at home. Running is just a means to get to a ball in order to execute the basics. Practice using this section in your living room and move to the ball's rhythm.

THE FOREHAND

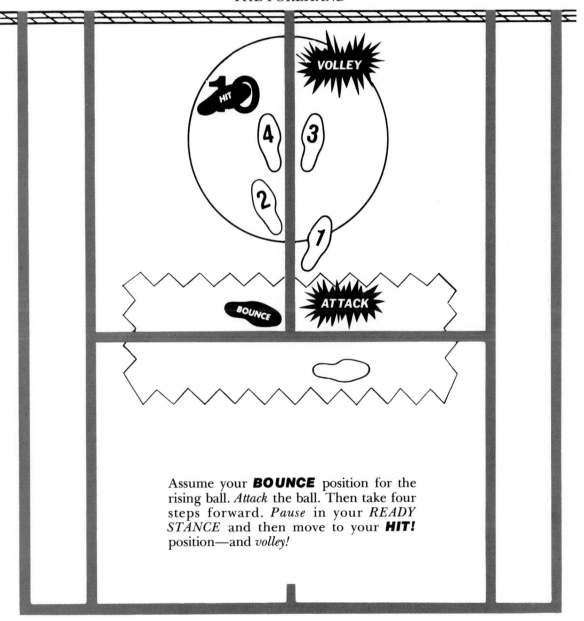

Assume your **BOUNCE** position for the rising ball. *Attack* the ball. Then take four steps forward. *Pause* in your *READY STANCE* and then move to your **HIT!** position—and *volley!*

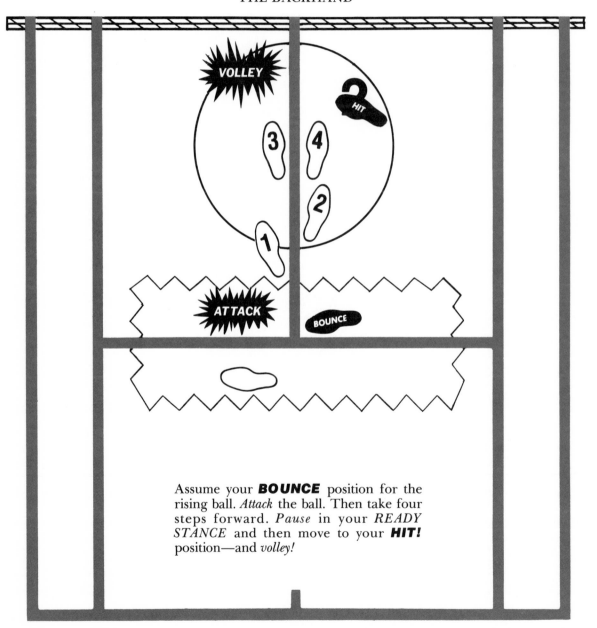

Assume your **BOUNCE** position for the rising ball. *Attack* the ball. Then take four steps forward. *Pause* in your *READY STANCE* and then move to your **HIT!** position—and *volley!*

STEP II

Chapter 11
THE TRANSITION

In order to move closer to the realities of tennis, you must now move out of the house. It has served you well. It has provided you a haven from the intimidations that inhibit free expression and prohibit the mind from working its will. You have shut out the general tension associated with embarrassment and fear, and in the absence of irrelevant movement and excessive strain you have developed an external guise whose promise is: with form there will soon follow function.

It is strange, but often it is those players with crude abilities who judge beginners. It is they who insist that beginners play with beginners and that they, "the tennis players," remain aloof and to themselves. Because of this unfortunate bias, the beginner plays the beginner—the blind lead the blind as beginners teach beginners to be beginners. The more serious student, intent on learning, is deprived of a proper "crack" at the ball.

It is the beginner who is most in need of practice and yet receives the least. It is *not* in the scheme of things that the beginner provide a beginner practice, for one cannot answer the basic need of the other—that a ball, once hit, be returned.

A rebound wall is the answer.

Tennis is for everyone, and walls are everywhere. They are the perfect partners for beginners who, having acquainted their bodies through exercise with classic tennis strokes, must now practice them. Only misguided ego would lead one onto a court without first encountering the ball.

You must teach the wall to play tennis! You must learn the ball's secrets together: how the ball bounces, why the ball spins. This is how it's done.

With your body turned to the Forehand side and with the appropriate grip, stand three feet in front of the wall. This will provide the wall a tennis touch. You begin near the end of the stroke (the **HIT!** position). With your wrist locked back, place your elbow well in front of your body as if reaching toward the wall. Keeping your elbow in close to your body will produce a "cuddling" effect in your right shoulder. As your left shoulder lowers, transfer your body weight to your left foot. You are now in the **HIT!** position. You must familiarize your body to this part of the stroke by executing the stroke repeatedly from it.

Now toss the ball upward. This will provide the ball a higher bounce. The ball's bounce must be high enough so that the racquet can be placed—not swung—for the ball must have a racquet to fall into.

An open-face racquet will soften the touch as your right shoulder pushes the ball up into the wall, rather than directly at it; and a game within a game is begun.

Your feet move about in quick time, as if dodging the possibility that the ball might get behind you. Your wrist stays firm. Your shoulder pushes and your elbow guides. Rhythm and touch become as much a part of the ball's movement as thought itself. Your elbow guides your wrist, and your wrist guides your hand in a harmonious body reflex.

Whether from a rebound wall in tennis, or from a childhood game of *Jacks,* the hand-eye coordination that attends this thought-free movement must be developed. Any deviate turn of the ball, any misjudgment of its movement, and all would be lost but for this body reflex. It preserves your initial intent—that the path of the stroke be perfect.

The wall *tosses,* the ball *bounces,* the racquet *hits!* The ball assumes its natural rhythm as confidence moves you back from the wall and your body takes on the image of STEP I.   Do not allow your body to forget what its muscles have remembered.

The **TOSS . . . BOUNCE . . . HIT!** rhythm is as real as your ability to create it.

Prepare before the ball bounces. Your body has developed a conditioned reflex that commands this. If you keep intact the **HIT!** position, then *is not the game's secret the bounce of the ball?* The bounce of the ball . . . *and time!*

You must develop the ability to prolong movement, to constrain body tension, until the ball has reached its hitting area: *The slower the ball's bounce—the slower your wrist rolls and the longer your body weight presses forward.* This is the torsion top players apply that tennis lovers the world over envy. They coil, and they uncoil—they snap at the ball. That's form personified.

The wall *tosses,* the ball *bounces,* the racquet *hits!* The force of the ball and your distance from it will determine whether the ball will be rising or falling— and what the relationship of the racquet head should be to it. You will either roll your wrist downward in a smooth, graceful manner (in order to brush up on the ball), or you will lock your wrist back in a static contraction and await the rise of the ball. In either case, your exercises have conditioned your body to remember and, with practice, your stroke will be perfect.

Footwork is a matter of common sense and comfort. The higher the ball's bounce, the more diagonal the step, until too high. It is then the body loses its poise and its contraction, and the pace that makes all strokes seem effortless is gone.

No stroke need go unpracticed. The RHYTHMETONICS exercise system was designed to make skill a habit. The wall will test that skill. It will evaluate your weaknesses and your strengths if, in turn, you lend it your patience.

In your mind's eye—see yourself! Throw off the initial shocks that may occur due to imperfect timing. *Let your mind watch your body move.* The ball itself will become incidental as in learning at home, and your body will be caught up in its rhythm.

STEP III

Courtesy of Flintkote DecoTurf

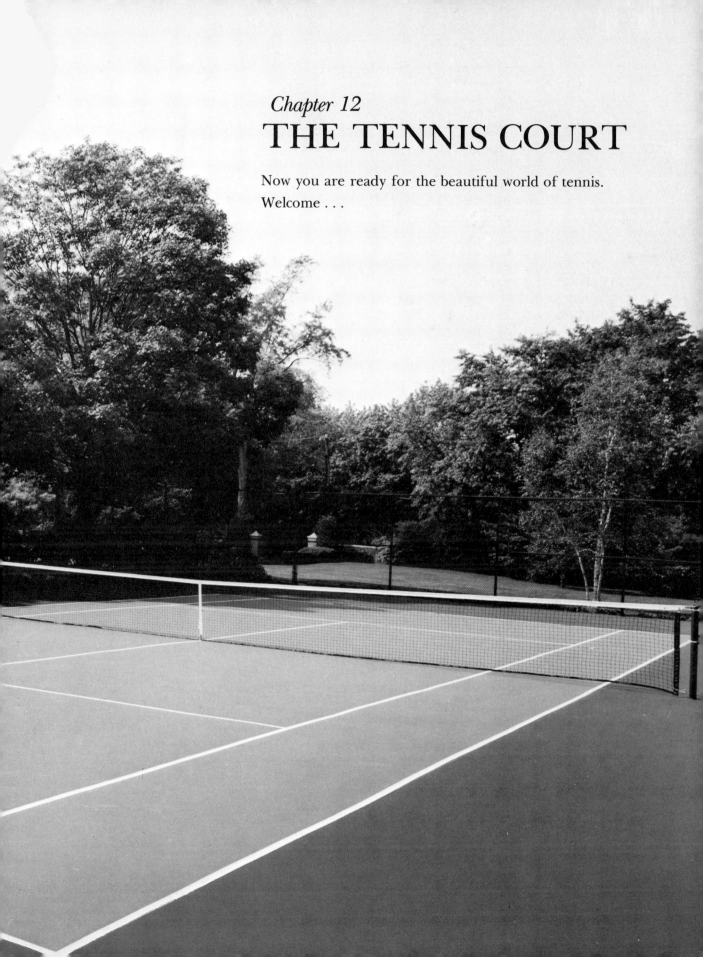

Chapter 12
THE TENNIS COURT

Now you are ready for the beautiful world of tennis.
Welcome . . .

THE COURT AND THE GAME

On the following page is a diagram of a tennis court showing its main features.

The Server and the Receiver stand on opposite sides of the net. The Server becomes the Receiver, and the Receiver becomes the Server, at the end of each game.

The Server must stand behind the baseline to deliver the Service; however, he may stand anywhere between the *AXIS* and sideline of the single's court in single's play, and the *AXIS* and the sideline of the double's court in double's play. The Server must begin each game by delivering the Serve from the right side of the court (1, see diagram) diagonally to the Receiver's Service box (2) and then on the next point from the left side (3) diagonally to the Receiver's box (4). The Server keeps alternating at the beginning of each point.

If the ball bounces on any line bounding the Receiver's Service box, it is considered fair play. If the first Serve does not bounce within the Receiver's Service box, it is called a fault and the Server is allowed a second Serve. If the Server fails again on the second Serve (*double-fault*), the point is awarded to the Receiver. If either Serve hits the top of the net before the ball bounces in the Receiver's box, that Serve is called a *let* and does not count; the Server is allowed to serve again. A *foot fault* is called if the Server touches the baseline with either foot throughout the delivery of the Serve.

The Receiver may stand anywhere on the Receiver's side of the court where it is convenient to return the Serve. However, the Receiver must allow the ball to bounce before returning it.

When a player wins his first point it is called *15*, his second point *30*, and his third *40*. The fourth point is called *game* unless both players have 3 points, or 40, in which case the score is tied and called *deuce*. When a player wins one point after deuce it is called *advantage*. If the same player wins the next point, he wins the game; if the other player wins the point, the score is again called deuce. The player scoring two consecutive points following the score of deuce wins the game.

A *set* is won when a player wins six games by a margin of two or more games. If five games are scored by both players, the score is called *five-all* and the player who then wins two consecutive games wins the set.

Two out of three sets, or three out of five sets, constitutes a *match*.

Zero in tennis is called *love*. When calling scores (for example, 0-15, 15-30, 40-15), the Server's score is always called first.